SOUL FOOD
WITH A TOUCH OF ESSENCE

SOUL FOOD

WITH A TOUCH OF ESSENCE

Food on the Go Book 2

L.F. Peterson

To order additional copies of this book, contact:
Xlibris
1-888-795-4274
www.Xlibris.com
Orders@Xlibris.com
794820

Contents

Bacon, Eggs & Toast

Makes 1 Serving

1 egg
2 slices of bacon
1-2 slices of bread
1 Tbsp. butter or margarine
Pinch of salt
Pinch of black pepper

Utensils

measuring spoons
butter knife
small bowl
skillet
spoon

    A. Wash hands
    B. Place all ingredients on table

    1. Place skillet on stove under medium heat. Add bacon, 1 slice at a time. Brown one side, turn over and brown the other side. When both sides are brown and lightly

crisp. Remove from skillet and place on a paper towel, on a plate.

2. To toast bread in an oven: Turn oven to broil. Use about ¾ of the Tbsp. of butter or margarine to lightly butter bread and set aside. The remaining margarine, set aside.

3. Crack an egg in a bowl and add a pinch of salt and pepper. Stir, mixing well.

4. Put the remaining butter or margarine in a skillet and place on the stove under medium heat. When butter melts add egg and stir until fluffy. Remove from heat.

5. Using oven, place bread underneath broiler and toast bread. Watch bread closely. Remove when lightly brown.

6. Using a toaster: Put bread in toaster, toast, butter and serve.

French Toast

Ingredients:
1 large egg
¼ c. milk
¼ tsp. cinnamon
1 tsp. butter or margarine
pinch of salt
2 slice of bread

Utensils:
measuring cup
measuring spoons
small bowl
large spoon
skillet

    A. Wash hands
    B. Place all ingredients on table
        1. Slightly beat eggs
        2. Add salt, cinnamon and milk.
        3. Mix and set aside.
        4. Put the margarine or butter in skillet and melt, using medium-low heat.

5. Dip bread into egg mixture, coating both sides. (Both slices)
6. Put bread into skillet, cook for about 1 minute, turn over and let cook about 1 more minute.
7. Remove from skillet and serve with jam or syrup.

Fluffy Eggs and Cheese

Ingredients:
2 eggs
¼ c. milk
1 pinch salt
1 pinch black pepper
¼ c. shredded cheese
1 t. butter or margarine

Utensils:
measuring cup
skillet
measuring spoons
bowl/knife

A. Wash hands.
B. Place all ingredients on table.
C. Shred cheese or cut into small pieces.
    1. In a medium bowl, slightly beat eggs.
    2. Add salt, pepper, milk and cheese. Mix together. Set aside.
    3. Put butter in skillet and melt under low heat.
    4. Add egg mixture, stirring slowly.
    5. When eggs are light and fluffy, remove from heat. Serve.

1. Put ham or sausage in skillet. Cook about 5 minutes or until lightly brown, using medium heat.
2. Add onion and green bell pepper. Cook until tender.
3. Remove from skillet, placing on paper towel to drain excess oil. Set aside.
4. In a bowl mix together eggs, milk, salt and pepper. Mix
5. Put skillet on low heat. Pour egg mixture and meat mix into skillet.
6. Cook about 1 minutes, flip over and cook other side about 1 minute or until fluffy. Fold, remove from skillet and serve.

Smothered Potatoes and Onions

Ingredients:
5 medium potatoes
1 c. vegetable oil
1 tsp. salt
½ tsp. black pepper
½ small onion (chopped)

Utensils:
measuring cup
measuring spoons
cutting board
skillet
large bowl

    A. Wash hands
    B. Place all ingredients on table
        1. Peel and wash potatoes.
        2. Put water in bowl, slice potatoes round about ¼ inch thick, place in bow of water and set aside.
        3. Put oil in skillet and place on stove using medium-low heat.
        4. When oil is hot add potatoes, salt, pepper and onions.

5. Cook about 7 minutes, turning until potatoes began to soften.
6. Drain off excess oil and place back on stove. Cover with lid to simmer about 8 minutes. Checking occasionally that potatoes don't burn.
7. Remove from heat, drain any oil remaining. Serve

Breakfast Meat

A. Large round sausages, smoked, Italian, etc.
   1. Put 3-4 cups of water into a pot and boil. Start to boil under high heat for about 5 minutes, then turn heat down to medium
   2. Cook for about 25 minutes or until sausage swells.
   3. Remove from pot, cut-up and serve.

B. Baking
   1. Place sausage in a pan and put into oven of 350 degrees.
   2. Bake for 30 minutes or until sausage swells.
   3. Remove from oven, cut-up and serve.

C. Breakfast sausages, small links or patties.
   1. Place skillet on stove and turn heat to medium-low.
   2. Place sausage, links or patties in skillet.
   3. Brown one side, turn over and brown the other side.
   4. Remove from skillet and place on a paper towel on a plate.
   5. Serve

D. Ham
   1. Put about 1/2 c. water in a skillet, when water starts to boil add ham and cook 2-3 minutes.

2. Remove from skillet and serve.

Fried Ham
1. Put 1 t. vegetable oil, butter or margarine in a skillet and place on stove. Turn heat to medium.
2. Add ham and cook for about 1 minute.
3. Turn to other side and cook another 1 minute or until lightly brown around edges.
4. Remove from skillet and place on paper towel on a plate.
5. Serve

Deviled Eggs

Ingredients:

6 eggs
½ tsp. mustard
2 Tbsp. Miracle Whip or Mayonnaise
1 ½ tsp. sweet pickle relish
1 tsp. minced onion
¼ tsp. paprika
1 pinches salt
2 pinches pepper

Utensils:

Measuring spoons
Large spoon
Mixing bowl
Cutting Knife
Pot

    A. Wash hands
    B. Place ingredients on table.

C. In a medium size pot add 2 cups of water and the eggs. Sprinkle with about ½ teaspoon salt and boil 15 to 20 minutes.

1. Drain water off eggs and add cold water.
2. Remove eggs from pot, peel, rinse and sit egg on a plate.
3. Cut eggs into halves;
4. Remove the yolk, put in mixing bowl and mash. Set egg whites back on plate and set aside.
5. Add mayonnaise or miracle whip, onions relish, mustard, salt and pepper to egg yolks in mixing bowl. Mix well.
6. Put about 1 teaspoon of egg mixture into each egg white half.
7. Sprinkle top with paprika. Serve.

Potato Salad

Ingredients:

6 to 8 potatoes

½ small green bell pepper (chopped)

1 hard- boiled egg

½ c. onion (chopped)

1 tsp. brown mustard

½ c. celery (chopped)

1 Tbsp. sugar

½ tsp. salt

3 Tbsp. dill pickle (chopped)

3 Tbsp. Mayonnaise

¼ c. dill pickle juice

¼ c. sweet pickle relish

Utensils:

measuring cup

large pot/bowl/spoon

measuring spoons

cutting board/knife

    A. Wash hands

    B. Place all ingredients on table.

1. Peel potatoes, wash and cut into chunks and put into a pot of cold water. Rinse egg off and place into pot with potatoes. Place on stove using medium heat. Cooking about 20 minutes or until potatoes are tender.
2. Remove potatoes and egg from stove and drain water. Place egg in a small bowl of cold water. Peel and chop.
3. Pour potatoes into a large bowl.
4. Mix in onions, celery and green pepper. Set aside for 2 minutes.
5. Add boil egg and remaining ingredients and mix well. If salad seems a little dry, add a little more mayonnaise or/and pickle juice. Too sour add a little sugar. Serve.

Grilled Cheese Sandwich

Ingredients:
2 slices of bread
1 slice sandwich cheese
1 Tbsp. butter or margarine

Utensils:
Measuring spoon
Spatula
skillet

A. Wash hands.
B. Place all ingredients on table.
   1. Melt butter or margarine in skillet, using medium-low heat.
   2. Brush butter or margarine on both sides of each slice of bread.
   3. Place 1 slice of bread in the skillet, then cheese. Place other slice of bread on top of cheese.
   4. Lightly brown. Turn sandwich over and brown other side.
   5. Remove sandwich from skillet. Serve.

Tuna Salad Sandwich

Ingredients:
2 (6 1/2 oz.) can tuna or
1 large can tuna
1 hard-boiled egg
1 Tbsp. sweet pickle relish
1 Tbsp. onion (chopped)
¼ c. cream cheese
½ stalk celery (chopped)
2 Tbsp. mayonnaise
pinch salt/pepper
8 slices of bread
2 Tbsp. sliced black olives

Utensils:
measuring spoons
can opener
Bowl/pot
cutting board
knife
fork

    A. Wash hands.
    B. Place all ingredients on table.

1. Open tuna and drain off excess water.
2. Place tuna into a bowl with cream cheese and mix until smooth.
3. Chop up boiled egg and add to tuna. Mix.
4. Add pickle relish, onion, celery, salt/pepper, black olives and mayonnaise. Mix well.
5. Spread tuna on bread and serve with chips.

Hungry Ham Sandwich

Ingredients:
2-3 slices ham
2 slices bread
1 slice Swiss cheese
1 slice sandwich cheese
lettuce
½ tsp. mustard
2 Tbsp. mayonnaise
1 slice red onion
pickles/or peppers
tomato

Utensils:
measuring spoons
spoon
plate
knife

    A. Wash hands
    B. Place all ingredients on table
        1. Slice tomato and onion, break lettuce and sit aside.
        2. Lightly toast bread.

3. Spread ½ of the mayonnaise on 1 piece of bread. The remaining mayonnaise on other slice of bread. Spread mustard on top.
4. Place 1 slice ham on bread, then Swiss cheese, lettuce, tomato, onion, pickles, sandwich cheese and remaining ham. Top off with other slice of bread. Serve with chips.

Note: Can substitute for Turkey, Roast beef, etc.

Homestyle Hamburger

Ingredients:
3 lb. ground beef
4 large hamburger buns (2 in a set)
4 slices onion
4 slices tomato
Shredded lettuce
1 Tbsp. salt or seasoning salt
1 Tbsp. black pepper
1 Tbsp. garlic powder
Miracle Whip or Mayonnaise
2 Tbsp. vegetable oil

Utensils:
measuring spoons
cutting board
spatula
large bowl
skillet
knife

    A. Wash hands.
    B. Place all ingredients on table.
    C. Rinse off lettuce and tomatoes.

1. Put ground beef in a bowl and break apart. Sprinkle salt, black pepper and garlic powder over meat and mix well and set aside.

2. Put oil in skillet and place on stove using medium-low heat.

3. Make 4 hamburger patties and place in skillet.

4. Cook for about 5 minutes, turn over and cook until meat is slightly brown. Pierce with fork, to make sure meat is done. Remove from skillet, place on paper towel to drain excess oil.

5. Toast buns, using a skillet or broiler in oven. Remove when slightly brown. Set aside.

6. Spread Miracle Whip or mustard on buns.

7. First place lettuce, tomato, onions. Top with hamburger patty. Then the other bun. Pickles (optional) Serve.

Battered Chicken Strips

Ingredients:
2- chicken breast
1 c. flour
1 tsp. salt or seasoned salt
1 tsp. garlic powder
2 c. vegetable oil
1 c. cold water
½ tsp. black pepper
bread crumbs (optional)

Utensils:
Measuring cup
Large bowl
measuring spoon
skillet/fork

    A. Wash hands.
    B. Place all ingredients on table.
        1. Wash chicken and cut into strips. Set aside.
        2. Mix together flour, salt, water, black pepper and garlic powder. Blend well.

3. Place skillet on stove with oil and heat under medium heat until hot. (Drip a little of batter into hot oil, will let u know its hot.)

4. While waiting for oil to get hot, dip chicken strips into batter. Put bread crumbs or flour in a pan. Roll chicken in it until covered, and set aside on paper towel until oil is hot.

5. Put chicken strips into hot oil, carefully, one at a time.

6. Brown on both sides. Remove from skillet, place on paper towel, to drain excess oil. Cool and serve.

Sweet and Sour Wing

Ingredients:

¼ c. soy sauce

1 Tbsp. minced garlic

¼ c. vinegar

1 c. brown sugar

8-12 chicken wings

1 c. pineapple juice

1 Tbsp. cornstarch

¼ c. water

½ tsp. pepper (your choice)

1 Tbsp. mustard

Utensils:

measuring cup

9x13 in. baking pan

Fork

measuring spoon

large bowl/spoon

    A. Wash hands.

    B. Place all ingredients on table.

    C. Pre-heat oven 350 degrees.

1. Rinse chicken wings, dry, put in baking pan and place in oven. Bake about 30 minutes

2. While chicken is baking, in a large bowl combine soy sauce, garlic, vinegar, brown sugar, pineapple juice, water, pepper, mustard, and cornstarch. Mix until well blended and smooth. Set aside.

3. Remove chicken from oven and drain off excess oil.

4. Pour sweet and sour mixture over chicken and place back into oven. Bake about 30 minutes more or until chicken is slightly brown on top. Remove, cool and serve.

Garlic Chicken and Pasta

Ingredients:
2 chicken breast
1 stalk celery (chopped)
½ small onion chopped
½ (16 oz. bag) egg noodles
1 chicken bouillon cube
¼ c. sour cream
3 c. water
4 gloves garlic (chopped)
1 carrot (oval slices)
¼ tsp. salt

Utensils:
measuring cup
cutting board/knife
measuring spoons
large pot/spoon

    A. Wash hands.
    B. Place all ingredients on table.
        1. Wash chicken, trim fat and cut into chunks. Set aside.
        2. In a pot (or sauce pan), put water, chicken and salt. Cook about 10 minutes using medium heat.

3. Add celery, onion and garlic.
4. Cook until vegetables are tender.
5. Stir in egg noodles and carrots. Cook until noodles are limp. Carrots are tender.
6. For thicker sauce: Use 1 Tbsp. flour, ½ c. milk and mix until smooth. Add to pasta and stir.
7. Stir in sour cream. Taste for seasoning. Serve hot.

Spaghetti

Ingredients:

3 lbs. ground beef

½ pkg. spaghetti (7 oz.)

½ small onion (chopped)

½ small green pepper (chopped)

1 c. mushroom(optional) chopped

3 tomato (chopped)or 8 oz. can stewed tomatoes (chopped)

4 cloves garlic (chopped)

8oz. can tomato sauce

1 c. water

1 Tbsp. chili powder

1 tsp salt/pepper

2 tsp. Italian seasoning

2 bay leaf

1 c. water

Utensils:

measuring cup

cutting board/knife

measuring spoons

large pot/large spoon

   A. Wash hands

B. Place all ingredients on table.

C. Rinse off vegetables.

1. Put ground beef in pot with about 3 c. water, break down, place on stove under medium heat and boil about 5 minutes. Drain off excess water.

2. Place on stove and add onions, green pepper, mushroom and garlic. Cook about 3 minutes, until vegetables are slightly tender.

3. Mix in water, tomato sauce, tomatoes, chili powder, salt/pepper, bay leaf and Italian seasoning. Mix well. Simmer under low heat about 15-20 minutes, stirring occasionally. If sauce is thick, add a cup of water. Simmer. Set aside.

4. Follow instruction on spaghetti box, cook spaghetti, rinse and add to meat sauce. Mix well. Simmer about 5 minutes. Remove from stove and serve.

Stuffed Marshmallow

Ingredients:
Large marshmallows
Strawberries
Melted chocolate

Utensils:
Cutting board/knife
Fork

    A. Wash hands.
    B. Place all ingredients on table.
1. Wash strawberries. Cut into thin strips or small pieces.
2. Using a for or small knife and put holes in marshmallow.
3. Fil holes with strawberries.
4. Toast or roast marshmallows until slightly brown.
5. Dip in chocolate. Cool and serve.

Spinach Dip

Ingredients:
1 (10 oz.) pkg. spinach small pkg. Knorr vegetable soup and dip mix
2 green onions (chopped)
1 (8oz.) can water chestnuts
¼ c. sour cream
¼ c. cream cheese
2 Tbsp. mayonnaise

Utensils:
measuring cup
cutting board
spoon
large bowl
knife

A. Wash hands
B. Place all ingredients on table.
1. Frozen spinach: Thaw, squeeze, dry and chop. For fresh spinach: Wash, dry and chop into small pieces. Set aside.
2. Drain water off water chestnuts, chop and set aside.

3. In a bowl mix together sour cream and cream cheese until smooth.
4. In a large bowl combine spinach, green onions, water chestnuts, sour cream, cream cheese, mayonnaise and soup mix.
5. Mix until well blended. Serve

Cream Cheese Dip

Ingredients:
1 (8 oz. pkg) cream cheese
½ 7 oz. pkg. Italian salad dressing mix
1/2 c. water chestnuts
¼ c. hot water

Utensils:
measuring cup
spoon
bowl
fork

    A. Wash hands.
    B. Place all ingredients on table.
        1. Chop water chestnuts into small pieces.
        2. In a bowl, add hot water to cream cheese, stir until smooth.
        3. Mix in well, salad dressing mix and water chestnuts. Serve.

Crab Dip

Ingredients:
1 (8 oz. pkg) cream cheese
3 Tbsp. minced onions
¼ c. mayonnaise
¼ c. celery (chopped)
1 ½ c crab meat
1 Tbsp. lime juice
1 Tbsp. lemon juice

Utensils:
measuring cup
spoon/knife
measuring spoon
bowl

A. Wash hands.
B. Place all ingredients on table.
   1. In a large bowl, add lemon juice, lime juice, cream cheese and blend until smooth.
   2. Add in mayonnaise, onions, celery and crab mead. Mix well. If stiff, add a little water. Serve with crackers.

Battered Chicken Strips

_____

Ingredients:

2- chicken breast

1 c. flour

1 tsp. salt or seasoned salt

1 tsp. garlic powder

2 c. vegetable oil

1 c. cold water

½ tsp. black pepper

bread crumbs (optional)

Utensils:

Measuring cup

Large bowl

measuring spoon

skillet/fork

    A. Wash hands.
    B. Place all ingredients on table.
        1. Wash chicken and cut into strips. Set aside.
        2. Mix together flour, salt, water, black pepper and garlic powder. Blend well.

3. Place skillet on stove with oil and heat under medium heat until hot. (Drip a little of batter into hot oil, will let u know its hot.)

4. While waiting for oil to get hot, dip chicken strips into batter. Put bread crumbs or flour in a pan. Roll chicken in it until covered, and set aside on paper towel until oil is hot.

5. Put chicken strips into hot oil, carefully, one at a time.

6. Brown on both sides. Remove from skillet, place on paper towel, to drain excess oil. Cool and serve.

Sweet Potato Pie

Ingredients:

2 lbs. sweet potato or yams

½ stick butter

2 tsp. nutmeg

1 egg

¼ c. evaporated milk

2 Tbsp. vanilla extract

2 Tbsp. flour

1-9 inch pie crust

Utensils:

measuring spoon

small bowl/large bowl

fork

can opener

large spoon

pot

    A. Wash hands.

    B. Place all ingredients on table.

    C. Preheat oven to 350 degrees.

        1. Wash potatoes, place in pot, cover with water. Place on stove under medium heat. Boil until tender.

2. Remove from heat, drain water off, peel potatoes and put in a large bowl. Mash.
3. Add butter while potatoes are hot. Mix well.
4. Slightly beat egg and add to mashed potatoes. Mix well.
5. Add milk, vanilla, and flour. Mix until smooth. Set aside.
6. Put pie shell into oven, 10 minutes or until slightly brown.
7. Remove pie shell from oven and pour potato mixture in it.
8. Place pie into oven for 25 minutes or until crust is browned.
9. Remove from oven. Cool and serve.

OLD FASHIONED APPLE PIE

Ingredients:

6-8 apples (peeled and sliced about ¼ inch thick).

1/2-2/3 cups of sugar (depending on sweetness desired)

1 T. lemon juice

3 T. Flour

¼ t. salt

2 t. nutmeg

1 t. cinnamon

1 t. vanilla

METHOD:

1. Preheat oven to 375 degrees F.
2. In a bowl combine apples, sugar, sugar flour, cinnamon, salt and nutmeg.
3. Mix well and pour into a 9" pie crust.
4. Top with pie crust. Brush with egg-wash mixed with about 1 Tbsp. butter (melted) and sprinkle with sugar(optional). Use a fork and poke holes in the top of crust, and place into the oven.
5. Bake until brown. About 30-40 minutes. Remove from oven, cool and serve.

7-Up Cake

Ingredients:
1 c. butter
1 c. margarine
6 eggs
3 c. flour
2 Tbsp. lemon extract
3 c. sugar
3 Tbsp. vanilla extract
1 c. 7-up

Utensils:
measuring cup
pound cake pan
mixer
measuring spoon
rubber spatula
mixing bowl

    A. Wash ands
    B. Place ingredients on table.
    C. Heat oven to 325 degrees.
    D. Oil and flour cake pan. Put flour between bottom and top of pan, so cake don't run out. Set aside.

1. Mix together butter and sugar. Beat until smooth and creamy. (about 15-20 minutes)
2. Add eggs one at a time. Mix well after each egg.
3. Add flour a little at a time, alternating with 7-up. Mix well.
4. Add vanilla and lemon extract. Mix well
5. Pour cake batter into cake pan, tap on table to even out cake.
6. Place in oven and bake about 1 ½ hours or until a golden brown on top and feels a little hard.
7. Remove from oven, cool and serve.

Heathful Smoothies

1. Turbo Express (Green)......Apples, cucumbers, pineapple, lime, spinach and avocado.
2. Carrot-Lemon and ginger .... (Orange) Carrots, apples, lemon and ginger.
3. Detox (Red).....Apples, carrots cucumber, broccoli, lemon, yellow bell pepper, beets and avocado.
4. Pineapple O.J. ..... Pineapple and orange juice.
5. Gingerade ...... (Yellow) Ginger, lemon, agave sweetner and water.
6. Everything green ...... (Green) Spinach, Kale, cucumber, broccoli, bananas or strawberry, coconut water or coconut milk. (All natural) Add what you like.
7. Must have a liquid to blend vegetables.
8. Make it yours!!!!!!